First published 2004 by Boxtree
an imprint of PanMacmillan Publishers Ltd.
20 New Wharf Road
London N1 9RR

www.panmacmillan.com

Associated companies throughout the world

ISBN 0 7522 7271 3

9 8 7 6 5

A CIP catalogue record for this book is
available from the British Library

Text by Giles Andreae
Illustrations by Janet Cronin
Printed and Bound in Hong Kong

a poem about
Falling in Love

It's funny how people say
"falling in love"
Cos I never felt any pain
And falling in love
Felt so lovely with you
That I think we should
do it again

a poem about

Love

When you love a person

You love all their
                different parts

But I just can't love
                the odour

Of your after-curry
                farts

a poem about
Snogging

Some people snog like a
watering can

And some like a washing
machine

Some people aren't really
snoggers at all

But you seem to snog
like a dream

a poem to say

You're Sexy

There's something I wanted
to tell you
I hope you don't mind
if I do
There's no-one who's half
as deliciously gorgeous
Or scrumptiously sexy as
you

a poem to say

I Love You

I thought I'd write a poem

Cos I wanted just to say

That I think you're
really scrumptious

And I love you more
each day

a poem about
Someone I Fancy

When I see someone I fancy

My face goes so blotchy
and red

That I want to crawl
under the carpet

And simply pretend that
I'm dead

a poem about
The One

The first time that I ever
met you
My body just sort of went
"wow
I know that's the person
I know that's the one!"
And you know - it's still
saying it now

a little
Secret Love Poem

I sometimes get this feeling

I hope it isn't wrong

But I want to take you
in my arms

And kiss you all night
long

♡

a poem about

That Tingly Feeling

It starts in the tips of
your fingers
And moves to the end of
your nose
And then it starts zooming
all over the place
Till it fills you right down
to your toes

a poem to say

You're Gorgeous

Sometimes as women get
older
Their bodies start showing
the weather
Their things start to droop
and to dangle
But you look more gorgeous
than ever!

a poem for

My Lover

I'd like to tell you something

I hope it won't offend

But if you weren't my
                     lover

You'd be my bestest
              friend

a poem about

Being with You

Some people love watching
football
And some like to play with
their cat
But my favourite thing
Is just being with you
And it's really as simple
as that

a poem about a
Love Bank

I wish there was a
Love Bank

Where we all had big
accounts

And we'd pay for things
with kisses

And give snogs for large
amounts

a poem to say

You're Wonderful

I know that it sounds
cheesy
But I'm telling you it's
true
It's fab to have a lover
Who's as wonderful as
💙 you

a poem about

Setting Me Free

I don't think I knew till
I met you
How happy a person can
be
It's just such a wonderful
feeling
So thank you for setting
me free

a little

Hugging Poem

I want you to know
That I think you are
                    great
And although I'm a bit
              of a mug
If you ever need me
I'll always be near
To come round and give you
              a hug

a poem to say

You're Scrumptious

However much money I pay
people
Some of them still won't
agree
That you're almost as
wonderfully scrumptiou
And gorgeously smashing
as me!

a poem about

Loving

Loving a person is easy
If only you've got the
right knack
-it's heaping your happiness
All over someone

Who loves heaping
happiness back

a poem for a

Gorgeous Man

I wanted just to tell you

That you're my perfect man

You're so handsome, cool

☆ and gorgeous

And I'm your biggest fa

a poem about

Ravishing You

'd like to go up to
the bedroom
And quietly turn down
the light
hen put on some beautiful
music
And ravish you madly
all night

a poem about

Not Doing It

When sometimes I don't
want to do it

Don't ask what I'm
sulking about

It doesn't mean anything
scary

It just means I'm really
fagged out

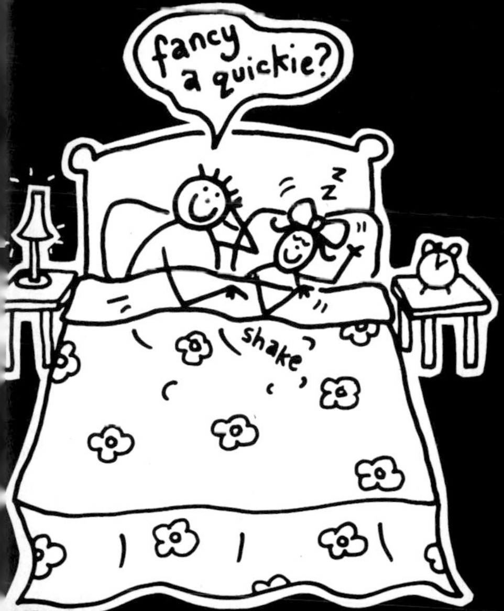
fancy a quickie?
zz
shake